JOHN DRANE

Christians

THROUGH THE AGES—AROUND THE WORLD

A LION BOOK

Text copyright © 1994 John Drane
This edition copyright © 1994 Lion Publishing

The author asserts the moral right
to be identified as the author of this work

Published by
Lion Publishing plc
Sandy Lane West, Oxford, England
ISBN 0 7459 2516 2
Albatross Books Pty Ltd
PO Box 320, Sutherland, NSW 2232, Australia
ISBN 0 7324 0744 3

First edition 1994
10 9 8 7 6 5 4 3 2 1

To Peter Graystone

Photographs
Andes Press Agency/Carlos Reyes: spreads 11 (top left), 14 (bottom right),
15 (centre right), 16 (top right)
Neil Beer: spreads 6 (top left), 10 (centre right), 11 (bottom right and title page), 12 (bottom left),
13 (centre left), 20 (centre left)
Suzanna Burton: spread 19 (top right)
Cephas Picture Library/H. Shearing: spread 15 (top left)
Ebenezer Pictures/Suzanna Burton: spread 19 (bottom left)
Keith Ellis: spreads 11 (centre right), 14 (bottom left)
Mary Evans Picture Library: spread 9 (top right)
Susan Hackett/CAFOD: spread 20 (bottom left)
Sonia Halliday Photographs: spreads 1 (top left), 7 (bottom left), 8 (top left),
/Andre Held spread 6 (bottom right), /Jane Taylor spread 8 (top right)
Jim Holmes/CAFOD: spread 19 (bottom right),
Hutchison Picture Library: /Bernard Régent spread 13 (bottom left),
/Liba Taylor spread 10 (top right)
Lion Publishing: spreads 3 (top left), 4 (bottom left), 9 (top left, centre left),
10 (top left), 12 (centre right), 18 (bottom right), 19 (bottom centre),
/Patricia Aithie spreads 1 (bottom right), and cover, 7 (top right), and cover,
14 (centre left), /David Alexander spreads 2 (top left, bottom right),
3 (centre right), 5 (bottom left), /David Townsend spreads 5 (top right), 17 (top left)
The following Lion Publishing photographs appear by courtesy of:
Eretz Israel Museum, Tel Aviv: spread 3 (centre left), and cover;
Biblical Resources Pilgrim Centre, Tantur: spread 5 (top left);
Rylands Library: spread 7 (centre left)
Reproduced by courtesy of the Trustees, The National Gallery, London: spread 9
(bottom right)
Novosti: spreads 11 (bottom left), 16 (bottom right), and cover
Rex Features: spread 18 (centre left)
Lois Rock: spread 18 (top right), and cover
Steve Rock: spread 19 (centre right)
Nicholas Rous: spreads 12 (bottom right), 18 (bottom left)
Alan Shepherd: spread 1 (bottom left)
Clifford Shirley: spreads 4 (centre left), 12 (top left), 13 (top left), 14 (top right),
15 (bottom left), 20 (bottom right)
Sean Sprague/CAFOD: spread 19 (centre left)
John Waterhouse: spread 12 (top right)
World Council of Churches: spread 12 (far right)
ZEFA: spreads 1 (top right), and cover, 15 (top right and bottom centre), 20 (top right)
/Ross Hamilton spread 2 (bottom left), /J. Henley spread 17 (bottom left)
/C. Krebs spread 17 (centre left) /Wiencke spread 16 (top left)

Acknowledgments

Illustrations
Diagrams by Oxford Illustrators
Cartoons by Kim Blundell

A catalogue record for this book is available
from the British Library

Printed and bound in Malaysia

CONTENTS

A WORLD OF CHRISTIANS

What comes to mind when you think of Christians? Perhaps it is a picture of a 'saint'—a famous Christian from days gone by, with a solemn expression and a halo of light around their head.

Or it might be a present-day Christian: perhaps hurrying towards a church building on a Sunday, carrying a book—the Bible, the special book of Christianity.

In fact you can't really tell just from the outside who the Christians are. Only a very few wear special clothes—the leaders of some church groups, for example, and some Christians who live in communities. But even though Christians may be hard to spot at a distance, there are in fact millions of them, and they are to be found in every country of the world.

More people in the world belong to the Christian church than to any other single organization.

There are more Christians today than there have ever been in the whole of history.

Margaret was a Scottish queen who helped the poor. After she died (1093) the church declared her a 'saint'—an example for Christians to follow.

WHAT IS A CHRISTIAN?

A Christian is, quite simply, someone who follows the teachings of a person called Jesus Christ who lived in a small country in the Roman Empire about 2,000 years ago. This book explains what Christians find so appealing about his teaching, and why they call it 'good news'.

WHAT IS A CHURCH?

Any group of Christians who meet together regularly is called a church. In this book you will discover more about different groups of Christians throughout the 2,000 years that churches have existed, and what makes them special.

WHERE ARE THE CHRISTIANS?

There are Christians in every nation of the world. The message of Christianity appeals to people from every kind of background: old and young, rich and poor, men and women.

Up until the last century, Christianity was mainly the religious faith of people in Europe and the places to which European explorers and emigrants went, especially North America and Australasia. In those

places, Christian customs and traditions were part of everyday life, and even people who didn't bother much about religion thought of themselves as 'Christian'. A hundred years ago, nine out of ten Christians were white western people.

Today, things are quite different. Six out of ten are neither white nor western. They live in places such as Africa, South America, Korea, the Philippines, Taiwan

and China, the country with the highest population in the world. The church is growing very rapidly in these countries. Church meetings in these places can be quite different from those in the West, as Christians use their own local traditions in music, drama and dance to celebrate what they believe.

Only a few people wear special clothes showing they are Christians. This picture shows a monk from a group called the Cistercians wearing a 'habit'. The habit looks old-fashioned . . . but the technology the monks use is not!

HOW MANY CHRISTIANS?

There are about two thousand million Christians today. One out of every three people in the world is a Christian.

More and more people are becoming Christians all the time. In Africa alone, almost 17,000 people become Christians every single day! Nearly 600 million Christians are fifteen years old or younger.

There are more Christians in today's world than there have ever been, and many of them are young people.

SOME THINGS NEVER CHANGE

Throughout the ages, the cross has been the main sign Christians have used to identify themselves. It is found in church buildings all over the world. A cross is sometimes carried around as part of a church meeting. Ordinary church members, as well as leaders, often wear a cross as a piece of jewellery.

The cross is a sign of death. Jesus was killed by being nailed on to a cross of wood (crucified) by the Romans. This method of execution was used for common criminals.

An intricately carved Celtic cross, more than 1,000 years old, at Eyam in England

The fish is another popular Christian sign. It too goes right back in history to the earliest days of the Christian church. They spoke Greek, and the Greek for 'fish' is *ichthus*. This reminded them of what they believed: *Iesous Christos Theou huios Soter* (Jesus Christ, God's Son, Saviour). The Christians used it as a secret sign to identify themselves, because at that time it could be dangerous to be known as a follower of Jesus.

IESOUS
CHRISTOS
THEOU
HUIOS
SOTER

The fish is a sign of life. Christians believe that Jesus was raised from death, and can bring new hope into the lives of ordinary people.

The cross and the fish both remind Christians of their founder: Jesus of Nazareth.

These two beliefs will always be at the centre of Christianity.

GOD'S PEOPLE

Are Christian beliefs unique? Any Christian would give a definite 'yes' to that question! There are things about Christianity that make it quite different from other religions.

However, it is important to remember that Christianity grew out of another religion—Judaism, the religion of the Jews. The story of that ancient faith is told in the Jewish special book, the Hebrew Bible. This forms the first part of the Christian Bible.

The very first story in the Bible is about creation. It tells about God making the world and everything in it. Most importantly, it explains the relationship between God and this world.

Jewish boys at their growing-up *bar mitzvah* ceremony show their understanding of the Hebrew Bible by reading some of it out loud. The round case contains a copy of the Jewish sacred writings, written by hand on a scroll.

People have a wonderful world to live in—but it is spoiled by things that harm and hurt. The Bible story about creation says that this is the result of people's turning away from God at the beginning.

1 PEOPLE, GOD AND PARADISE

There was a time when everything in God's world was perfect. The first people—whom the story calls Adam and Eve—lived peacefully together and as friends of God.

But things soon changed. The people began to live as *they* wanted. They no longer cared about God. Nor did they care if the things they did hurt other people.

That story about the beginning of the world describes how the world has been ever since. People are still more concerned about themselves than about others—and that leads to all kinds of unhappiness—quarrelling in families, bullying at school, unkindness between neighbours, and wars between nations.

2 PUTTING THINGS RIGHT

People turned away from God to act as they wanted. But God still loved the world and its people.

God chose the family of Abraham for a special job and made a solemn promise to them: Abraham and his family would follow God and discover God's care and concern for them, and for all the generations to come. This family became the nation called Israel.

At one time, the nation was enslaved by the evil king of Egypt. But God acted to help them. Led by a man named Moses they were able to escape and make a new life for themselves in their own land. On the way there, God gave the people laws, including the Ten Commandments. The people could show their love for God by keeping these laws. The laws would also help them to create a community in which everyone could enjoy justice and peace.

But from the beginning it was clear that it would be very hard to keep the law. The people also had to remember to ask God for forgiveness when they had done wrong. God was willing to forgive, but would not tolerate disobedience. However, once again the people began to take God's love for granted. They forgot God's laws.

These are the ten great laws that God gave to the Jewish people. To this day, they influence lawmaking in many countries around the world.

3 RIGHT AND WRONG

God is always on the side of right, and could not ignore people's selfish disobedience. The nation of Israel suffered at the hands of many enemies, and it seemed as if God's promises would never come true.

The Ten Commandments

I am the Lord your God who brought you out of Egypt, where you were slaves. Worship no god but me.

Do not make images and then bow down and worship them as if they were gods. And don't worship any other idols.

Do not use my name wrongly.

Keep one day in seven—the Sabbath—special. On that day, no one is to work.

Respect your father and your mother.

Do not murder.

Husbands and wives: be completely loyal in your love for each other.

Do not steal.

Do not tell lies to get people into trouble.

Do not want for yourself something that belongs to another person.

Based on Exodus 20:1–17

4 NEW PROMISES

God did not forget the nation of Israel, nor the promises made to them. Instead, God gave new promises to David, the first of a new line of kings who ruled the people from their capital city, Jerusalem.

But still the people disobeyed God's laws. Those who were loyal to God began to think that God would need to send a special king—a Messiah—if things were ever to change.

Still, God chose many people to be special messengers— 'prophets'. They reminded the people about God's laws, and about God's promise to send a special king to rescue them.

That became the great hope of the Jewish people.

5 A SPECIAL KING

Christians believe that God's special king—the Messiah—has come. They believe that Jesus was the Messiah, and that he came to begin the process of putting things right in the world, and to give people a way to escape from selfish wrongdoing.

Jerusalem has been an important place for the Jewish people for thousands of years. It was here that they first built a temple where they could worship God. A Muslim mosque with a golden dome now stands on the site of the temple.

The Christian faith began with a person called Jesus. He was born 2,000 years ago to Mary, an unmarried teenager from a small town called Nazareth in the land of Palestine. She and her fiancé Joseph had travelled to Bethlehem, and it was there that Jesus was born.

Stories about his birth say that he was not the son of a human father but the son of God. God sent angel messengers to tell people that this child was special.

The region where Nazareth and Bethlehem are found is called Israel today. In Jesus' day, the country was treated as just a rather unimportant part of the great Roman Empire. The Roman emperor Augustus ruled all the lands around the Mediterranean Sea.

Christmas cards often depict well-known scenes from the stories of Jesus' birth. These stories are found in two books of the Bible—those by Matthew and Luke.

Augustus, the Roman emperor at the time Jesus was born

Bethlehem today: sheep still graze on the hillsides around the town.

JESUS GROWS UP

Jesus did not attract much attention while he was growing up. He lived in a simple home. As a boy he would have learned the family trade.

The Bible tells how, when he was twelve, he went with his family to the temple in Jerusalem, the capital city. While there, he struck up a discussion with some of the religious leaders in the temple, and amazed them with his understanding of God. There was *something* remarkable about him. But after that, he went home to live a normal life like the other children growing up in Nazareth.

He would have begun regular work—as a general builder like Joseph—when he was a teenager. Not surprisingly, his best friends were other ordinary working people. Several were fishermen who fished from small boats on nearby Lake Galilee.

But it was the things he said and did as a grown man that had such an enormous effect . . .

PALESTINE IN JESUS' DAY

Jesus was born in a village called Bethlehem and grew up in Nazareth. As a boy he travelled with his parents to the capital, Jerusalem. Later he visited the same region to tell people about God.

Caesarea Philippi ●
Where Peter says he believes Jesus is God's promised rescuer

Capernaum
Where Jesus heals the Roman centurion's servant

a ●
re Jesus turns
r into wine

LAKE GALILEE
Where Jesus calms a storm

● Nazareth
Where Jesus grows up

River Jordan

Jericho
Where Jesus heals a blind man
●

rusalem
here Jesus spends the
t week of his life

1lehem,
re Jesus is born

DEAD SEA

Fishing on Lake Galilee. Scenes like this were familiar to Jesus and his closest followers.

0   25   50 kilometres

WHAT'S IN A NAME?

'Jesus' is an ordinary first name. Like many first names, it has a meaning—and it means 'rescuer'. Stories about Jesus' birth say that the angel who told Mary that her child would be the son of God also told her to give her son this name. The Bible story says the name was a sign that Jesus would rescue people from the wrongdoing that makes the world such an unhappy place.

Jesus is often called 'Jesus Christ'.

'Christ' is a title, and people only began to use it about Jesus when he started his work of telling people about God. It comes from a Greek word that means 'anointed'. The Hebrew word *Messiah* has the same meaning. It was used for someone who had been anointed to be king. The people who used it believed that Jesus was the special king God had promised to send.

WHAT YEAR IS IT?

The system of counting years in the western calendar is linked to the time of Jesus' birth. Events before that are commonly dated 'BC', meaning 'before Christ', and those that come after are dated 'AD'. These letters stand for *anno domini*, Latin words meaning 'in the year of the Lord'.

Nowadays, the letters BCE, 'before the Common Era' and

CE, 'Common Era', are sometimes used instead.

Actually, we now know that Jesus was not born in the year 0, at exactly the point when BC ends and AD begins, but about four years earlier (in 4 BC). Scholars in the Middle Ages got their sums wrong when they worked it all out, and it would be too complicated to change it now.

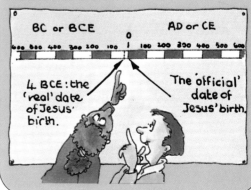

A MESSAGE OF LOVE

Love. Everybody needs it—from the time they are born to when they are very old. They need it when things are going well, and even more when things are not. Jesus showed people a love that met their needs.

It was when he was about thirty years old that Jesus began his 'public' work. He went from place to place, speaking to anyone who would listen to him.

As people heard him, they realized he was saying new and exciting things. He spoke of God's love for all, and he claimed that anyone could get to know God as a personal friend.

But Jesus did more than speak. He actually showed God's love in action, by curing those who were blind, healing those who were lame and even, it was said, bringing people who had died back to life.

And he always had a special concern for those who had been badly treated and who were looked down on and rejected. Jesus' message was for everyone, but especially those who were hurting in some way.

Within a short time, crowds would come hurrying when they heard he was in their area.

Jesus looked just like an ordinary man. Yet whenever he spoke about God, crowds gathered. This open-air Christian meeting follows his example.

LIGHT IN THE DARK

Jesus said that his teaching was like a light that would show people the right way to live. Not surprisingly, the people who knew their lives were in a mess were eager to find out more. Those who thought they were doing the right things by themselves felt insulted.

An oil lamp, like those used in Jesus' time to light the home at night.

FRIENDS

Jesus chose some special friends to go with him as he went about teaching.

One day he was walking on a beach, on the shores of Lake Galilee, when he saw some fishermen. They were good workers, and Jesus knew he needed people like that to help him. 'I see you're good at catching fish,' he said. 'I need people with your skills to share God's love with others: will you come and join me?'

And so he got his first disciples: two brothers, Simon (whom Jesus renamed Peter—'the rock') and Andrew.

Next came James and John—now there were two sets of brothers, who were all fishermen. Then there was Matthew, who was a tax collector before he met Jesus, and who had dishonestly overcharged a lot of people.

Others are little more than names to us today: Thomas, Thaddaeus, Philip, Bartholomew, another James, another Simon, and finally Judas Iscariot (who eventually

Jesus often called 'disreputable' people to follow him.

betrayed Jesus to his enemies). These people are often called the twelve disciples—a word that means followers or students.

But as well as these twelve especially close friends, Jesus invited all sorts of people to follow him—not just religious types, but ordinary women and men.

Thousands of people followed him wherever he went. Many of them were not quite respectable—they did the wrong sort of jobs for that. They were surprised that anyone religious should be interested in them. But Jesus had many new things to teach them.

They learned that God sees people differently from the way we see each other: God is not so much concerned with the way people look, or how much money they have as with the kind of people they really are.

Once they understood that, Jesus invited those who followed him to change their lives and serve God—by loving others in the same way they had been loved.

ENEMIES

Not everyone liked Jesus. Some religious leaders were jealous, because Jesus had more followers than they did.

This was hardly surprising. The religious leaders had spent their lives studying the laws that God had given to their people centuries before and trying to work out every last detail of how people should live. As you can imagine, it was hard to keep all the rules—though many of them did—and many ordinary people felt that their religious leaders looked down on them.

Jesus, however, seemed to want to turn everything upside down. He hinted that God loved people who recognized their faults; and that God was not impressed by those who spent all their lives trying hard to do good and attending religious services.

Before long, the leaders challenged Jesus about all this. In reply he claimed that he knew God better than they did! He even went about forgiving people

for what they had done wrong, and saying he did so on behalf of God. What did he mean? Was he himself God?

If making these claims had been all he did, it would have been easy to think that he was crazy. But it wasn't just words. The leaders could see as well as anyone else that Jesus obviously had some special powers, because he healed people of all kinds of illnesses. Could anyone but God do that kind of thing?

All this made Jesus' enemies very uneasy. They eventually managed to convince enough people to agree with them to get Jesus arrested and put on trial.

WHO CAN CURE ILLNESS?

It was plain to everyone who saw Jesus heal people that he had power. But where did he get it from? People could not agree, as this story shows.

One day when Jesus was walking along with his disciples, they saw a man who had been born blind. Jesus rubbed some mud on the man's eyes . . . and for the first time ever, he could see.

The religious leaders heard about the healing, and they were most upset. For one thing, Jesus had broken one of the religious laws by healing the man on the Sabbath: and God's laws said no one should do any work on that day. So that made

Jesus a sinner, didn't it?

But the problem was, the man had really been healed. And when they spoke to him, he gave them a very clear answer:

'I don't know if Jesus is a sinner or not,' he said. 'All I know is this: I was blind and now I see.'

The religious leaders were really

angry with him, but he wouldn't change his mind.

'Look,' he said. 'We know that God doesn't do what sinners want. And since the world began, no one has been able to give a blind person their sight back. If Jesus didn't come from God, he wouldn't be able to do things like this.'

Well, the leaders

told the man he couldn't come to any more religious meetings with them . . . but he could still see, and he believed in Jesus.

From John 9

Many of the people who knew Jesus loved him because of the good things he did. You might think that only good things should happen to good people. Indeed, one year when Jesus came to Jerusalem to celebrate the Jewish festival called Passover, crowds cheered and waved as he rode in on a donkey. But then the story took a nasty turn.

Jesus seemed to know that this would happen. When he shared the simple Passover meal of bread and wine with his disciples, he told them so. As he shared the bread, he told them that his body was going to be broken just as the bread was broken. And when he shared the wine, he told them to remember that his blood was going to be shed just as the wine was poured out.

Later that night, in an olive grove in the city of Jerusalem, Jesus was arrested. His enemies, the religious leaders, had not dared to arrest him when he was surrounded by the crowds who were

eager to hear him. But one of his own disciples, Judas Iscariot, had told those leaders where they could find him alone with just a few of his close friends.

Jesus was put on trial before the Roman governor, Pontius Pilate.

Jesus and his disciples would have shared their last meal together in a room similar to this.

WHAT CRIME?

The Jewish religious leaders who had arrested Jesus could not stand the way he spoke about God with such authority. But only the Roman authorities could pass the death sentence on a criminal—and the Roman authorities weren't bothered about a wandering preacher.

But the Jewish people had for centuries been longing for a special king—a 'Messiah' or 'Christ'. Some were expecting a king who would overthrow the Romans—and many thought Jesus was this 'king of the Jews'.

Pontius Pilate's job was to make sure that the Emperor was

obeyed in his part of the Empire. He knew he had to show that rebels would not be tolerated.

So Jesus was crucified as a common criminal, on a hill called Calvary just outside Jerusalem. His disciples were shattered, and they went into hiding. But they were soon hearing some amazing stories.

The tomb of Herod the Great, king when Jesus was born, gives a clear idea of what Jesus' tomb would have looked like.

THE FIRST EASTER

Women who went to Jesus' grave a couple of days after his death found it was empty. His body was gone—and they were sure he was alive again.

A husband and wife walking home late at night were joined by a stranger. Because it was late they invited him in—and, as they began supper, they recognized that the stranger was Jesus, alive again. He certainly surprised them but they had no doubt it was really him.

Afterwards, many of his disciples saw Jesus alive again. They talked and even had a meal together.

Jesus' coming alive after he had been killed is called the resurrection.

The sun was rising over Jerusalem when the women went to Jesus' tomb . . . and found that Jesus' body had gone!

MAKING SENSE OF IT ALL

Christians believe a number of things about Jesus' death and resurrection:

● One of the first Christians, Paul, wrote that on the cross, 'Christ died for our sins'. The Jews had been used to sacrificing animals as a way of asking for God's forgiveness. By dying in this way, Jesus himself accounted for all the wrong there had ever been in the whole world.

● Christians believe that what Jesus did brings them forgiveness and a new start. God also gives them power to overcome the weakness in themselves that leads to wrongdoing.

● Those who are oppressed—who suffer because of the wrong that other people do to them—

are attracted by the fact that Jesus was also persecuted and murdered unjustly.

● Those who suffer know that Jesus understands how they feel.

● Jesus' resurrection gives reality to the hope of a life after death. This is a comfort to people who know they are dying, or who have watched people they love die.

● People are encouraged to know that real success and happiness is to do with knowing God

and doing what God wants—as Jesus did. It has nothing to do with having an important job or being rich and famous.

● It seems only right that Jesus should come back to life if he did not deserve to die. The resurrection shows people that God does indeed put right things that are wrong. People are attracted to a God who is just and fair.

Did Jesus Really Come Alive?

'Surely Jesus didn't really rise from the dead, did he?'

That was the question on everyone's lips. But the disciples were sure the answer was 'yes'.

None of them expected Jesus to come to life again. They were as astonished as everyone else.

They knew they weren't just dreaming. They had met Jesus, and they had seen that the grave was empty.

The disciples hadn't stolen his body. They were ready to die for their belief in his resurrection, and they would hardly have done

that for something they knew to be a lie. Jesus' enemies couldn't have stolen his body. If they had, they would have produced it and stopped the stories of his disciples at once.

The disciples knew that the resurrected Jesus had a different kind of body from the Jesus they had known. It was definitely the same person—but now he could pass through walls and doors, as well as do ordinary things like eating food. They soon concluded that Jesus was unique. He really was the Messiah, and his teaching was true—and because he was alive in a new way, he would be with them for ever.

GOOD NEWS TO SHARE

Jesus had come alive again! At first, Jesus' disciples were confused and uncertain about what to do next. But Jesus gave them a special job to do. Soon they received new strength and power from him to do it. They described this as the presence of God within them—'the Holy Spirit'.

Christians today continue the work Jesus gave his first followers—telling others the news about him and about how they can be part of God's family.

Banners proclaim that 'Jesus lives' and 'God is love'.

THE HOLY SPIRIT

Christians know the 'Holy Spirit' as a person: the Spirit of God, constantly present with them, encouraging and helping them to do what pleases God. Paul wrote that *the Spirit produces love, joy, peace, patience, kindness,* *goodness, faithfulness, gentleness, and self-control.* Galatians 5:22

This is rather different from how people usually are!

A SPECIAL JOB

When Jesus met with his disciples after the resurrection, he told them to spread his message all over the world—starting in their own province of Judea before moving out through the rest of the Roman Empire. It was a daunting challenge. How could ordinary people like them ever be bold enough to do that?

PENTECOST

Jesus was crucified during the Jewish religious festival of Passover. Forty days later, he said goodbye to his disciples. They said that he was taken up into heaven.

Ten days after that came the Jewish festival of Pentecost. While praying together behind closed doors on that day, the disciples suddenly sensed something like a strong wind blowing over them, and what seemed like flames of fire came down and touched them. They began to speak, but not in their own language. And when they went into the street, they were able to talk with people from faraway places in their own native languages.

Everyone was amazed—including the disciples. But from that day forward, things were never the same again. When Peter explained what had happened, 3,000 people were convinced that what he told them about Jesus Christ was true. They asked Peter what they should do, and he said this: *'Each one of you must turn away from your sins and be baptized in the name of Jesus Christ, so that your sins will be forgiven; and you will receive God's gift, the Holy Spirit.'* Acts 2:38

They became Christians there and then.

Wherever they went, the friends of Jesus attracted a great following.

From this point on they were called 'apostles'—from a Greek word meaning 'sent'—because they were sent out on a great mission.

INTO ALL THE WORLD

The disciples did as Jesus had told them, and took his message across the world. One of the early converts to Christianity was a Jewish religious teacher called Saul (in Hebrew) or Paul (in Greek). He travelled all over the Roman Empire, setting up new groups of Christians wherever he went.

Less than twenty years after Jesus' death and resurrection, there was a strong church even in Rome, the capital of the Empire.

By the year 100, Christians could be found all around the Empire, winning new converts to their faith in Jesus. People in every land found that the Christian message met their needs:

● It helped to explain what life is all about.

● It put them right with God and gave them a new start.

● It showed them how people should live.

● The Holy Spirit—the presence of God in them—gave them power to live as God wants.

CHRISTIANS AND JEWS

Jesus and his first disciples were all Jews. So were all the earliest Christians. Some supposed that anyone who wanted to follow Jesus would have to join the Jewish religion before they could be proper Christians.

But it was not long before they saw that the only thing needed to be a Christian was to believe in Jesus, and trust his teachings.

That meant that Jews and non-Jews (sometimes called 'Gentiles') should treat each other with equal respect.

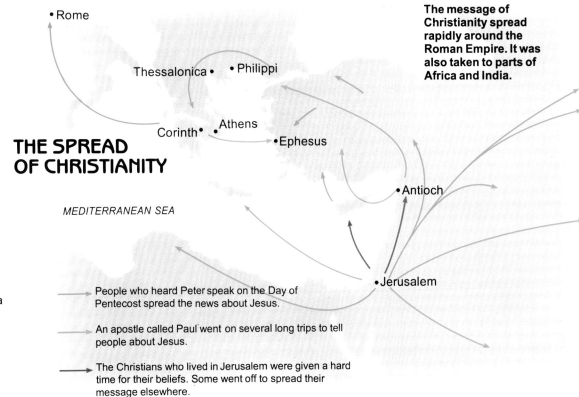

The message of Christianity spread rapidly around the Roman Empire. It was also taken to parts of Africa and India.

• Rome

Thessalonica •   • Philippi

Corinth •   • Athens

• Ephesus

THE SPREAD OF CHRISTIANITY

MEDITERRANEAN SEA

• Antioch

• Jerusalem

People who heard Peter speak on the Day of Pentecost spread the news about Jesus.

An apostle called Paul went on several long trips to tell people about Jesus.

The Christians who lived in Jerusalem were given a hard time for their beliefs. Some went off to spread their message elsewhere.

ROME IN A RAGE

It was hard to be a Christian in the early days—as it often has been since. The leaders were suspicious of Christians: what were these strange new ways of worship they had, so unlike the way Romans worshipped their gods? And why would they not join the army? The Emperor needed a strong army to help keep control of the countries the Romans had conquered.

Because they were hated, Christians were frequently thrown into prison and beaten up.

The mad Emperor Nero sent many Christians to fight wild animals as a form of circus entertainment. He had others dipped in tar and set on fire to light the driveway to his own house.

He had Peter crucified upside down, and Paul beheaded.

But more and more people became Christians all the time! One reason must have been that their lives were different, and that they showed their love for each other in practical ways. Indeed, one writer, who did not agree with Christianity, had to admit as much: 'See how they love one another.'

The first Christians were known for caring for each other. Paul wrote: 'Share your belongings with your needy fellow Christians, and open your home to strangers (Romans 13:13).

WRITING IT DOWN

How do people today know anything about events that took place 2,000 years ago—or earlier than that? It is because different people at different times felt it was important to write down what they knew about God, about God's people and about Jesus. That way, these things would not be forgotten. The result is a remarkable collection of books, which Christians call the Bible.

The Bible consists of sixty-six different books. These contain many stories, from the one about the creation to the stories of Jesus and his disciples. There are other types of writing, too: poems, and history books, and lists of laws, for example. By reading the Bible, Christians learn something of their history, and discover how God wants them to live.

THE OLD TESTAMENT

Before Jesus was born, his people, the Jews, already had their own Bible. This was the Hebrew Bible. It contains the first thirty-nine books of the Christian Bible: the part called the Old Testament.

This was the Bible Jesus knew. It was originally written in the Hebrew language, but the first Christians usually read a Greek translation of it called the Septuagint. This was produced in Egypt a century or two before the time of Jesus.

The Pentateuch					History												Poetry and wisdom					The Prophets																
GENESIS	EXODUS	LEVITICUS	NUMBERS	DEUTERONOMY	JOSHUA	JUDGES	RUTH	1 SAMUEL	2 SAMUEL	1 KINGS	2 KINGS	1 CHRONICLES	2 CHRONICLES	EZRA	NEHEMIAH	ESTHER	JOB	PSALMS	PROVERBS	ECCLESIASTES	SONG OF SOLOMON	ISAIAH	JEREMIAH	LAMENTATIONS	EZEKIEL	DANIEL	HOSEA	JOEL	AMOS	OBADIAH	JONAH	MICAH	NAHUM	HABAKKUK	ZEPHANIAH	HAGGAI	ZECHARIAH	MALACHI

THE BIBLE THROUGH THE AGES

The Bible was written by ordinary people. Yet it is no ordinary book. Many people have found that God seems to speak to them through it in special ways. As they think about the words, they really do learn more and more about God and about how they should respond to God's love. And that is why Christians want people to read it for themselves.

Soon after the books of the New Testament were written (in Greek), they were translated into other languages used in the Roman Empire, such as Coptic, Syriac, Latin, Gothic, Armenian and Georgian.

Since then, the Bible has become the most-translated book in the whole world, and the most-translated parts of it can be obtained in more than 2,000 languages.

For the first 1,400 years of Christianity, the Bible, like all other books, had to be copied out by hand, but when printing was developed in Europe the Bible was the first book to be printed.

Thousands of people have given up all they owned just to be able to have their own copy, and every day millions throughout the world eagerly read it, because they find that what it says guides and inspires them in their daily living.

Here is part of an 'illuminated' manuscript made by monks in the Middle Ages. The first letter has been beautifully decorated. The text is in Latin.

THE NEW TESTAMENT

The books of the Old Testament (on the left) and the New Testament (on the right). Some of these books—such as the story of Jonah, and the letter of James—are just a few pages long. Others, such as Genesis, are about as long as a typical junior novel.

The New Testament contains twenty-seven books that were written by the earliest Christians. The first churches were scattered in different countries—hundreds of miles apart. However, they could keep in touch very well by writing letters to each other. These letters were the first parts of the New Testament to be written. Later, the stories of Jesus were also written down, which meant people all over the world could read them and get to know about Jesus' life and teaching.

DID YOU KNOW?

A stained glass picture tells a Bible story: God speaking to a man named Moses, calling him to be a leader of God's people. In the Middle Ages, pictures like this helped people who could not read to learn Bible stories.

Gospels and Acts — The Letters

| MATTHEW | MARK | LUKE | JOHN | ACTS | ROMANS | 1 CORINTHIANS | 2 CORINTHIANS | GALATIANS | EPHESIANS | PHILIPPIANS | COLOSSIANS | 1 THESSALONIANS | 2 THESSALONIANS | 1 TIMOTHY | 2 TIMOTHY | TITUS | PHILEMON | HEBREWS | JAMES | 1 PETER | 2 PETER | 1 JOHN | 2 JOHN | 3 JOHN | JUDE | REVELATION |

The Gospels contain stories about Jesus, and accounts of his teaching. They were written by his followers during the fifty years after his death and resurrection, and were named after people who either wrote them or supplied much of the information: Matthew, Mark, Luke and John.

The Acts of the Apostles (or **Acts** for short) is the story of the church and it comes next after the Gospels. It was written by Luke, as a follow-up story to his Gospel—to tell what Jesus' disciples (now called apostles) did after his death and resurrection.

The Letters are sometimes called 'epistles'. They were real letters, written by leaders of the early churches to keep in touch with their friends, often in reply to letters the churches had sent them. They contain advice about many things: for example, they talk about important Christian beliefs, such as the resurrection of Jesus and what it means, but they also give advice on everyday affairs such as what kind of food Christians should eat. Most were written by just one person—Paul—but other church leaders also wrote some.

Revelation is the last book in the New Testament. It reports a series of visions received by a man called John. In them he saw how God would finally defeat the powers of evil and put right all the wrongs of the world.

From early times, Christians were eager to have copies of the stories of Jesus, written by the people who knew him. This is a fragment of a copy of the Gospel written by John. It is written in Greek on a piece of papyrus.

Here is one piece of advice to Christians, from the letter Paul wrote to the Ephesians:

Children, obey your parents in the Lord, for this is right ...

Fathers, do not exasperate your children; instead, bring them up in the training and instruction of the Lord.

Ephesians 6:1, 4

In the year 312 came a very important event: the Emperor Constantine himself became a Christian. He ordered that Christianity should now be the official faith of the whole Roman Empire.

For the next thousand years, Christianity shaped what happened throughout the continent of Europe—as it was eventually to shape the whole world.

CHRISTIAN BELIEFS

As the number of Christians grew, there were more and more ideas about what followers of Jesus should believe. The church leaders had to think hard about which beliefs were right, and agreed with what Jesus and the apostles had taught.

Then they had to explain them in such a way that they could not be misunderstood or twisted. The statements they put together are called 'creeds'. They spelled out as clearly as possible what Christians believed.

One of the earliest and best-known 'creeds' is the Apostles' Creed. It is still said aloud by Christians in many churches around the world.

The Apostles' Creed

I believe in God the Father almighty,
maker of heaven and earth.
I believe in Jesus Christ, God's only Son,
    our Lord.
He was conceived by the power of the
    Holy Spirit,
and born of the Virgin Mary.
He suffered under Pontius Pilate,
was crucified, died and was buried.
He descended to the dead.
On the third day he rose again.
He ascended into heaven,
and is seated at the right hand of God
    the Father.
He will come again to judge the living
    and the dead.
I believe in the Holy Spirit,
the holy catholic church,
the communion of saints,
the forgiveness of sins,
the resurrection of the body,
and the life everlasting.

A SPECIAL WAY OF LIFE

Around the time that Christianity became officially approved in the Roman Empire, some Christians felt it was important to live a way that was quite different from that of other people in society. Some went off to wilderness areas to live as hermits, where they could live simply and spend their lives praying to God and reading the Bible.

Others decided to live in communities— men as monks in monasteries, women as nuns in convents. Often, they farmed the land so they could provide for all their own needs. They spent a lot of time studying the Bible, worshipping God and praying.

Some communities also provided practical help for people, such as caring for people in special need—the sick, the very poor, and the elderly.

Over the years, many of these communities prospered, and there was time to produce beautiful books, including decorated copies of the Bible, and great works of art.

Constantine, the Roman emperor who made Christianity the 'official' religion of the Roman Empire in 312CE. This dramatic mural, painted over a thousand years later, recalls how he became a Christian after he had a powerful vision of the cross of Jesus.

THE CHURCH GOES TO WAR

In the year 610 of the Western calendar, the prophet Muhammad founded the new religion of Islam, and it soon began to spread into many countries. In places like Spain, Christians managed to live together in peace with the followers of Islam, called Muslims. In other places, such as North Africa, Christianity almost disappeared.

The church leaders in Rome saw Islam as a great threat, and many kings of Western Europe shared their concern. When they knew that Muslims had control of the Holy Land of Palestine, where Jesus had lived, they felt they must fight to get it back.

In four 'crusades' from 1095 to 1204, thousands of European soldiers formed great armies to go to Palestine. The kings who led them believed they were fighting for their faith in God. Of course, they were also looking for extra power and lands for themselves.

Christians have never quite been able to agree whether war is ever right. Jesus advised his disciples not to take up arms . . . but sometimes, as the Crusaders must have felt, it seemed that Christianity was under attack and should be protected. Over the centuries, Christians have often gone to war. Still, many Christians believe there is a better way of solving problems than fighting about them. Certainly, Christians down the ages have bitterly regretted the Crusades, which have spoiled the relationship between Muslims and Christians ever since.

The Church of the Holy Sepulchre (tomb) in Jerusalem was built by the Crusaders.

CHRISTIAN WRITERS

As Christians tried to explain their faith in convincing ways, some people became known for their writings about the faith: these Christian philosophers helped many people to understand their faith better. Always they talked of Jesus, and the difference he made to their own lives.

A prayer by Augustine, a famous Christian writer who lived in Hippo, North Africa, in the fourth century.

O God,
you have made us
for yourself, and
our hearts are
restless until they
find rest in you.

EAST AND WEST

From early times, there were important churches in two cities: Constantinople and Rome. They each affected the way the churches in countries near them were organized: things like who should lead a church, and how worship should happen.

Over the years, the two branches of the church developed in different ways. Eventually they could no longer agree with each other. In the eleventh century they officially split: the Roman Catholic church in the West, and the Eastern Orthodox church in the East.

They are still separate today.

EUROPE: THE EASTERN AND WESTERN CHURCHES

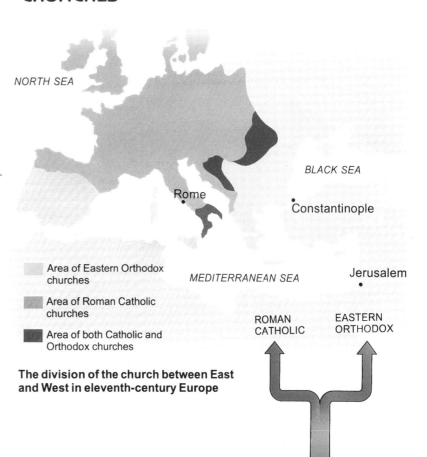

NORTH SEA

BLACK SEA

Rome

Constantinople

MEDITERRANEAN SEA

Jerusalem

Area of Eastern Orthodox churches

Area of Roman Catholic churches

Area of both Catholic and Orthodox churches

ROMAN CATHOLIC

EASTERN ORTHODOX

The division of the church between East and West in eleventh-century Europe

During the Middle Ages, the church in Europe had a great deal of power. The leader of the church in Rome, the pope, was able to tell kings how they should rule. Throughout society, other church leaders all had an important say in how people should live.

Many good things happened during the centuries when the church was powerful. But as church leaders became greedy for money and power, their selfishness made them forget Jesus' teachings. Eventually this led to a great split.

EDUCATION

The church was very wealthy and it developed schools and universities. Some of the great scholars in them wrote important books about their faith. Christians today still value these very highly. Thomas Aquinas, Thomas à Kempis and Desiderius Erasmus are three of the most famous of these scholars.

How to live as Jesus wants

Try to be patient in bearing with the failings and weaknesses of other people, whatever they may be. You too have many faults which others have to endure.

The Imitation of Christ
by Thomas à Kempis

Dame Julian of Norwich (about 1342–1413) wrote this prayer about her experience of God's love.

O God,
as truly as you are our father,
so just as truly you are our mother.
We thank you, God our father,
for your strength and goodness.
We thank you, God our mother,
for the closeness of your caring.
O God, we thank you for the great love
you have for each one of us.

Julian of Norwich

Delicate fan vaulting for the ceiling of King's College Chapel in Cambridge, England (fifteenth century). Throughout the ages, Christian artists and craftspeople have used their skills to honour the God who gave them special talents.

Milan Cathedral, Italy, is a spectacular example of the cathedral building of the Middle Ages—and shows how rich and powerful the church had become.

Inside a Protestant church—Great Church, Haarlem (Holland). In the Dutch Reformed Church, the congregation sat around the pulpit to listen to the sermon from the preacher.

QUARRELS AND DISAGREEMENTS

In spite of all the splendour of the church in the Middle Ages, it had many problems. One of the most famous examples of wrongdoing was the practice of selling 'indulgences': in return for money, people could have a priest say that their sins were forgiven, and that they would get a better place in heaven.

Jesus had never said anything of the kind! Those who read the Bible knew this, and felt they had to protest.

Problems like this led to a great deal of arguing among people in the church. In the turmoil, many Christians were persecuted by those who had different views, and even put to death.

Protestants believed that people should be able to read the Bible in their own language instead of priests telling them what the Latin meant. In England, John Wyclif's translation was plain enough for farm workers to read.

The Reformation

A turning-point in the history of Christianity came in the sixteenth century, when a monk named Martin Luther became so bothered about the difference between the teaching of the church and the teaching of the Bible that he nailed a notice to the door of his church in Wittenberg, Germany, pointing out some of the questions he wanted to discuss. As a result of going public with his ideas, Luther was no longer allowed to be a member of the Roman Catholic church. This happened in 1521.

It was the beginning of a new movement, in which people who had strong beliefs about what was wrong in the Catholic church left it to form their own. From what people now call the Reformation, a totally new kind of church emerged: the Protestant churches, formed by people who protested against the ways of the existing church. Their two most famous leaders were the German, Martin Luther (1483–1546), and a Frenchman, John Calvin (1509–1564).

Many people warmed to the teaching of people like Luther and Calvin. Soon Protestantism became a third great section of the church—alongside the Orthodox and the Roman Catholic churches.

Martin Luther was a leading figure in the move to reform the church in the sixteenth century.

PROTESTANTS

Those Christians who left the Catholic Church—Protestants—claimed they were putting the Bible back in the centre of church life. In the process, they got rid of anything they thought was not in the Bible.

They got rid of the colourful and ornate decorations in churches, and banned both the grand ceremonies and the lively music, dance and drama that had been used to worship God.

They insisted that the only way to know about God was through reading the Bible. Anything that could possibly distract people from this had to be thrown out.

Worship became very severe and serious. Instead of wearing brightly-coloured robes, Protestant ministers dressed in black and expected their people to sit and listen to their long talks (sermons) which now dominated worship.

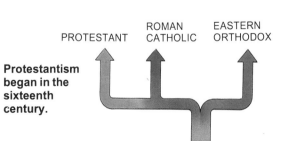

Protestantism began in the sixteenth century.

PROTESTANT | ROMAN CATHOLIC | EASTERN ORTHODOX

CHRISTIANITY GOES WORLDWIDE

After the Reformation, Protestant churches were formed in great numbers through the whole of Europe. In the centuries that followed, both Catholics and Protestants from Europe took their faith to other countries around the world.

In the twentieth century, churches all over the world have been changed yet again: this time by the Pentecostal movement. Many of the churches in the developing world today are Pentecostal.

The special clothes worn by the leaders of this African church are in a style worn by some church leaders in Europe. They are a reminder that some African churches were founded by European missionaries.

MISSIONARIES

The church has always had missionaries. Jesus told his followers to go out and spread the faith 'to the ends of the earth'. Since that time, Christians have been keen to tell other people the good news about Jesus that has brought them freedom and joy.

As the great age of exploration and discovery got under way in the fifteenth century, Christians realized that the ends of the earth included countries they had not known about! Missionary monks and nuns came forward who wanted to share their faith with the peoples in the countries that Europeans were visiting for the first time.

However, the eighteenth and nineteenth centuries were the great age of missionaries, both Catholic and Protestant. They sometimes made mistakes as they went to other countries to tell people about their faith. For example, some imagined that to live like Europeans was the same thing as being Christian!

But many did manage to show people the kind of love that Jesus had showed. And people responded. Fine schools and hospitals were founded by Christians, as well as relief organizations that still work among the victims of war and famine.

Today, missionaries from other continents are taking the gospel back to Europe again.

CHRISTIANITY: A WORLD FAITH

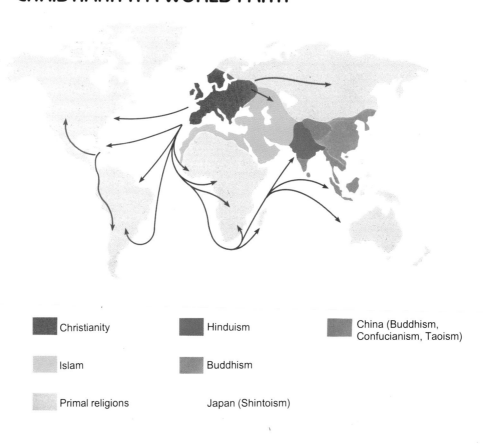

Christianity	Hinduism	China (Buddhism, Confucianism, Taoism)
Islam	Buddhism	
Primal religions	Japan (Shintoism)	

Catholics first took Christianity to South America some 400 years ago. Here a priest and a nun lead a service at a mission station in Bolivia.

A BRAVE MISSIONARY

England, 1932. Gladys Aylward felt that God really wanted her to be a missionary, telling people in China about Christianity. But she had just been turned down for this work. And she had almost no money.

She prayed: 'Oh God! Here's me, here's my Bible, here's my money, use us, God, use us.'

Amazingly, she managed to get enough money to go to China. To her surprise, she was soon given a job by the Chinese leaders: she was to visit homes making sure people were obeying a new law: from now on they were not to bind up little girls' feet to keep them unnaturally small, but let them grow. As she did her work, she had opportunities to tell people stories about Jesus.

During the Second World War, China was invaded. Refugees had to flee from the fighting, and Gladys led a group of more than 100 children on a long journey across the mountains to safety.

Later, she worked with children on the Chinese island of Taiwan. Life was difficult, and people tried to cheat her, but she worked on doing good to others.

She said: 'I believe that God has called you and me and it is not to walk as other people have walked in a nice rosy way, but just along the way he walked to Calvary . . . one day we will know and understand why.'

THE PENTECOSTALS

The Pentecostal churches are the fourth great strand of the world church today.

The modern Pentecostal movement started in 1906, in a church in Azusa Street, Los Angeles. The Christians there were having the same amazing experiences as Jesus' disciples on the Day of Pentecost (see spread 6). They spoke in languages they had never known before, and found they were able to heal people 'in the name of Jesus'. It seemed as if the stories of the New Testament were repeating themselves all over again.

When dramatic events like this happen, it's easy for many people to see something of the power of God. That is perhaps why the Pentecostal movement is so appealing in the modern world.

Today there are Pentecostal churches everywhere. In fact, there are estimated to be about 410 million

Christians who are Pentecostal.

Another word for Pentecostal is charismatic, from the Greek word *charisma*, which means 'gift'. This is because the new abilities people experience depend on the *gift* of the Holy Spirit.

The Yoido Full Gospel Church in Korea is Pentecostal. It has the largest congregation of any church in the world: 850,000 people.

Pentecostalism became the fourth great strand of the church in the twentieth century.

PENTECOSTAL   PROTESTANT   ROMAN CATHOLIC   EASTERN ORTHODOX

There are well over 20,000 different Christian groups—or denominations, as they are called—in the world today. They all worship Jesus Christ, and try to live by his teachings. But there are many ways of doing this.

THE ORTHODOX

Orthodox Christians trace their history to the great church of Constantinople which separated from the church of Rome back in the eleventh century.

Orthodox services are very dramatic, with much use of incense, holy pictures called icons, and light from candles. It would be impossible to have a service without a priest.

Orthodox Christians are found in Eastern Europe and Greece, as well as many other countries to which people from these lands have emigrated.

ROMAN CATHOLICS

A priest leads the service in a Roman Catholic church.

The Roman Catholic Church has its headquarters at the Vatican in Rome. From here, the pope directs

A NEW DIRECTION

Many Catholic and Protestant churches are now attracted by Pentecostal ideas. The new kinds of experiences that Pentecostals enjoy has shown them ways in which they could know more about God and help each other more too.

and leads the church. The pope is the successor to the bishops of Rome going right back to the time of Peter. The Roman Catholic Church claims the longest history of any Christian church. This was the church that Martin Luther—and many others—left at the time of the Reformation. Since then, the Roman church has itself been reformed. One important change in recent times (a result of the Second Vatican Council held in 1964 in Rome, which all the bishops attended) is that the church services are not always in Latin, but in the language the local people speak. Another is new interest in getting people to read the Bible and pray regularly. In this way they take responsibility for learning about their faith. Also, ordinary members of the congregation are allowed to take an important part in the church services.

The main service is called the Mass in which the people celebrate Jesus Christ's death and resurrection by sharing bread and wine.

Catholic churches are often beautifully decorated with paintings and stained glass windows. The service may be sung to music, and often the priest burns incense, to symbolize how the prayers of the people go to God. These things help make the event very special.

The splendour of an Orthodox service is clear to see in this special thanksgiving ceremony held at the Patriarchal Cathedral of the Epiphany in Moscow.

THE EPISCOPALIANS

Episcopalians belong to the Anglican Communion—the group of churches which began with the Church of England.

Back in 1534, when the English king Henry VIII wanted to divorce his wife, the pope refused to allow it. When Henry disobeyed him, the pope declared that Henry was no longer a member of the Roman Catholic church. So Henry set up his own church, but he didn't change his beliefs. The split from Rome had more to do with politics than faith.

As a result, some Episcopalian churches today seem very similar to Roman Catholic churches. However, because they are not under the authority of the pope, others are much more like Protestant churches.

These churches are strongest in Britain, the USA, and in those countries that were once part of the British Empire.

PROTESTANTS

Many groups of Christians call themselves Protestants. They include Lutherans, Presbyterians, Methodists and Baptists.

The teaching of Protestant churches is rooted in the Bible, and church traditions are not as important as in the Roman Catholic and Orthodox churches. Individual members are encouraged to learn about their faith by regular prayer and Bible study, and to work out what they *think* about their faith. They do not believe that the Bible's teaching supports the idea that only specially qualified 'priests' can deal directly with God. 'Ordinary' Christians in Protestant churches may have the opportunity to preach or teach. However, many Protestant churches do have ministers, who take a leading role in teaching and in organizing what goes on in the church.

A Protestant minister. Some Protestant ministers wear distinctive clothes when they lead church services; others do not.

PENTECOSTALS

Pentecostals believe much the same things as other Protestants, but there is an important difference. Pentecostals believe that some of the dramatic things that happened in the early church and are clearly described in the Bible are still very important today. These dramatic things include miraculous healings, or being suddenly able to speak in other languages ('tongues').

This, say the Pentecostals, was how God worked in the life of Jesus and his disciples. Modern Christians can expect to *experience* God in the same way.

They are less formal than the older churches, and instead of being led only by the official leaders—priests and ministers—ordinary members of the church are able to play an important part. They may organize the worship services, for example, or give the talk. The actual worship is more obviously joyful and enthusiastic, with lots of music and dance, as well as speaking in tongues and healing during services.

Enthusiastic singing at a Pentecostal gathering.

The church is people: people who see themselves as part of God's family. This family includes people of all ages and interests, and all different nationalities.

The way their church is organized, what they do when they meet together, and the type of building they meet in are far less important than their faith in Jesus Christ!

Christians want to use their special skills for God. Learning how to play music for worshipping God is one way of doing this.

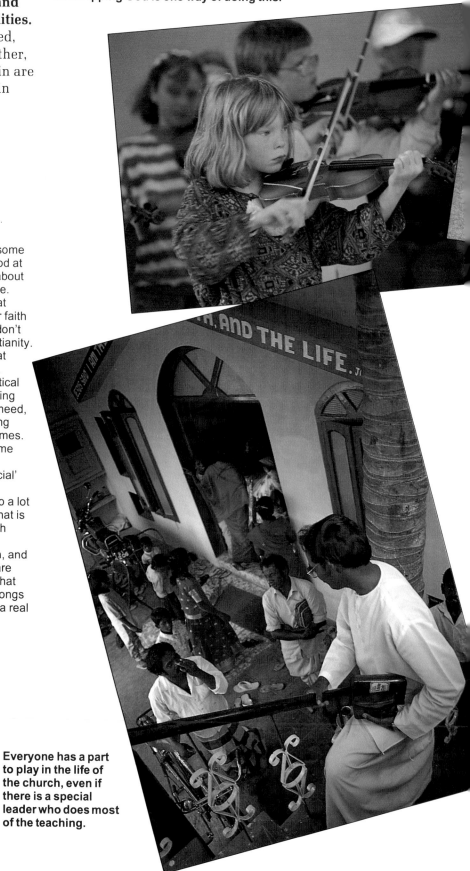

GOD'S WORKERS

In the New Testament, the apostle Paul describes the church as 'the body of Christ'. Christians have to do the work that God wants in this world, which is to help other people see God's love.

As a result, Christians should work together in the way the human body works. Hands, eyes, feet and ears each have different jobs, but a body cannot work properly without any of them.

In the church, people may be very different: men and women, young and old; people from different backgrounds and from different countries; people who have a lot of money and power and others who do not ... and all these Christians may be good at doing different things. But they all need one another.

For example, some are especially good at teaching people about God from the Bible. Others are good at talking about their faith with people who don't know about Christianity. Others are good at organizing things. Others have practical skills, such as taking care of people in need, perhaps welcoming them into their homes.

In the past, some churches have expected the 'official' leader of the congregation to do a lot of this work. But that is not how the church worked when Christianity began, and today Christians are finding out again that *everyone* who belongs to the church has a real part to play.

Everyone has a part to play in the life of the church, even if there is a special leader who does most of the teaching.

Christians need to encourage one another. Making the trip to do this can be as simple as going along the street. But you need a plane to visit this group of Christians in Papua New Guinea.

Christian friends help each other by reading the Bible together.

Christians meet to learn from each other about their faith.

PUTTING ASIDE DIFFERENCES

As soon as Christians remember that they are all part of God's family, they see how much they need one another and should work together—to show their love for God and for each other, and to share that love with others.

The World Council of Churches was formed in 1948 as a way of encouraging this. Churches of all kinds now regularly work together in lots of ways. The Orthodox, Protestants and Pentecostals are all members of the World Council of Churches, together with many of the newer churches from the developing world.

The Roman Catholics did not join in 1948, but since the Second Vatican Council (in 1964) they have worked very closely with all these other Christians.

Every country in the world has its own national organization to help Christians work together. This is the 'ecumenical movement'.

WHAT DO CHRISTIANS HAVE IN COMMON?

'Jesus is Lord.' This simple statement was one of the earliest ways in which Christians summed up their understanding of Jesus. Christians today, including the members of the World Council of Churches, all share this belief. It means two things:

● In the Old Testament, God was given the title 'the Lord'. When Christians say 'Jesus is Lord', they mean that Jesus is one with God.

● In the Roman Empire, the emperor was 'the Lord': he had to be obeyed. The first Christians called Jesus 'Lord' to acknowledge that they would obey *him*. And that is what Christians still mean: what Jesus said and did is an example for them to follow.

In all the churches of the world, Jesus is always at the centre of what Christians believe and how they live.

THROUGH THE DOOR

Just as the family home says something about the family that lives there, so church buildings say something about the Christians who built them, and about those who still meet in them.

A simple church interior that is clearly loved and cared for, in Lapland

Jesus often spoke of God's concern for the poor. This simple building provides a meeting place for Christians in a poor area of India.

CHURCH DETECTIVE

The cross is very important in Christianity, and Christians often include a cross somewhere in their church buildings. If you visit a church, look to see if there is a cross anywhere. It might be . . .

● a large wooden cross fixed on the wall

● in the shape of the building

● in a stained glass window

● as a small ornament

● on a banner.

Look for other symbols of Christianity: the fish, for example (see spread 1), or a dove, which is a symbol of the Holy Spirit.

A great view of what is going on and spectacular surroundings make the Crystal Cathedral in California, USA, a breathtaking location for Christian celebrations.

A church on this plan is 'in the round' so that everyone can see each other and focus on the centre.

These pictures are of churches from different traditions. Look for the following in each:

- where the bread and wine is laid out
- where the leaders stand to give a talk
- where people can sit or kneel to pray
- where musicians can lead the people in singing
- where there is room for other activities—a procession, dance, or drama
- where the people might meet to chat to each other before or after the main service
- what special arrangements there are to have a baptism—a washing with water.

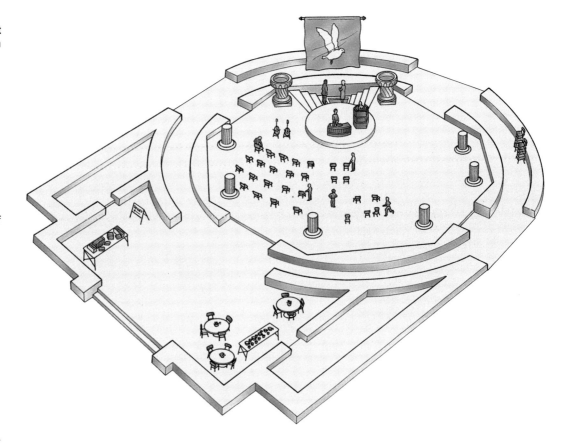

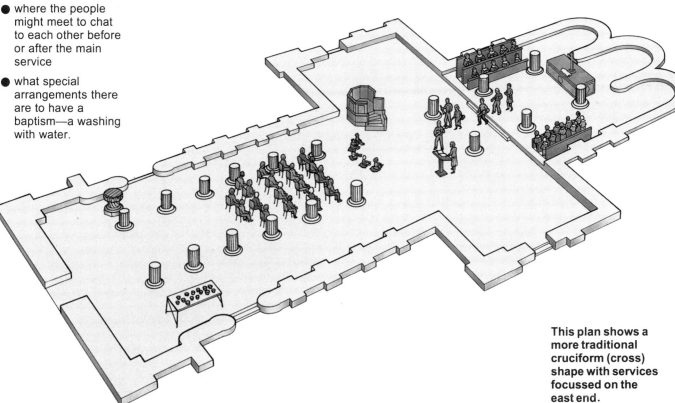

This plan shows a more traditional cruciform (cross) shape with services focussed on the east end.

The special day when Christians meet for worship is Sunday, the day of Christ's resurrection. Many different things happen in worship, for there are church services to suit all tastes.

Worship in a Quaker service can mean sitting in total silence for an hour. In a Pentecostal service, there could be singing and dancing all the way through!

Sometimes ministers and priests lead what happens from the front. At others, the people (the 'congregation') may help. In some churches the meeting may break into small groups, to pray and talk together.

In their services, as well as by themselves, Christians often repeat the prayer Jesus taught his disciples. Since the early days of Christianity, it has become the custom to end the prayer with these words:

For the kingdom, the power, and the glory are yours now and for ever. Amen.

Dancers taking part in a Christian worship service

The Lord's Prayer

Our Father in heaven,
hallowed be your name,
your kingdom come,
your will be done,
on earth as in heaven.
Give us today our daily bread.
Forgive us our sins
as we forgive those who sin against us.
Lead us not into temptation
but deliver us from evil.

Matthew 6:9–13

Young Christians singing praises to God with a rousing cheer

THE SERVICE

In everyday speech, performing a service means doing something for someone else. In a service of worship, people give their worship to God—they express their love and commitment—and they encourage one another. A typical service would include the following:

Praise

Christians have many reasons for praising God. Singing is a favourite way to express praise. The music is often provided by an organ, but you might find a small group of musicians, or even a whole orchestra. In a Salvation Army service, you would hear a brass band.

There could also be a choir—but there will always be a chance for everyone to join in the singing.

Dance may also be used, giving people the opportunity to use their whole body to show their love for God: praise does not always have to be in words.

Prayer

One of the most wonderful things Jesus told his disciples was that they could speak to God at any time. He gave them a prayer—called the Lord's Prayer—as a model, so they would know the kind of things to say.

Prayer can be a form of spoken praise. It can also be giving thanks for all that God has done. And it will include 'intercession', inviting God to take special care of particular people or situations—asking God to 'bless' them.

Reading the Bible

There may be a reading from the Old Testament or one of the New Testament letters: there will probably be one from the Gospels.

Saying the Creed

It is helpful for Christians to have a quick way to sum up what they believe. Many Christians say a Creed, a statement of their beliefs, to remind themselves of the faith they share (see spread 8).

Sharing bread and wine

Before his death, Jesus shared bread and wine with his disciples. He told them to go on doing this with each other, to remember his death (see page 5). Nearly all groups of Christians have done so regularly ever since. Depending on the denomination, it may be called the Mass, Communion, Eucharist, the Lord's Supper or the Breaking of Bread.

Learning about the faith

A leader—usually a priest or minister—may give a talk, sometimes called a sermon or homily. It might be an explanation of a particular Bible reading, or a more general talk to teach Christians how to keep following Jesus.

Fellowship and friendship

Christians meet their friends in church. After the service, they may have a drink or a meal together. In many churches, they will greet one another at a special point during the service. This is called 'sharing the peace', because they say the words, 'The peace of God be with you.'

Sharing a cup of wine at communion is a feature of many church services.

Part of a church service may be spent in quiet prayer.

All over the world, people have their own special ways of marking important family occasions—celebrating the different stages all people go through as they grow up, starting with birth, and ending with death. Christians have special ceremonies to mark these events.

The details of how people celebrate can vary quite a bit from one group of Christians to another. Local traditions also affect how things are done—for example, a Christian wedding in India is not the same as one in England.

But always Christians will make a point of expressing their faith in Jesus Christ.

WELCOMING NEW CHRISTIANS

Human families celebrate when they gain a new member of the family—most usually, when a baby is born. Christians have ways of welcoming new members of God's family.

In some cases, the welcome involves giving thanks to God for the safe arrival of the baby, and giving the parents a chance to say aloud that they promise to teach their child about Jesus.

In other churches, part of this welcome is baptism. The sign of the cross is made in water (or sometimes oil) on the baby's forehead, to show that the new baby is now part of the family of God. Then water is poured over the baby's head.

In Orthodox churches the baby is actually dipped in water!

Young people who have been already baptized can make the promise to follow Christ at a ceremony called Confirmation.

The church leaders will welcome the young person into the church, either by laying hands on their head and praying for them, or offering their hand in fellowship.

When children grow up they will have the chance to declare their faith in Jesus for themselves.

Of course, grown-ups who haven't been baptized can become Christians. Often, when adults are baptized they are dipped in water—for which a large baptistry or a river is needed!

A grown-up declares she wants to be a follower of Jesus, and is baptized—in the sea!

In some churches, babies and young children are baptized with just a sprinkling of water from a font.

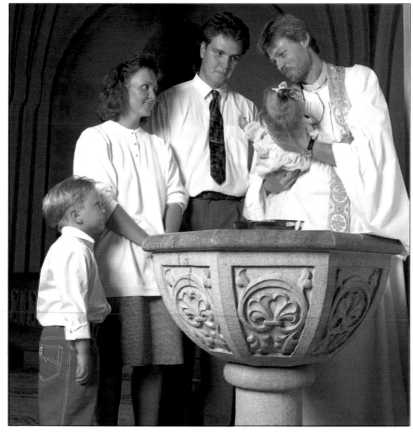

GETTING MARRIED

Finding a partner and becoming a family is an important part of life for many grown-ups. In some countries, it is usual for the couple to agree to marry because they love each other. In others, the parents of young people will try to arrange a suitable match.

In either case, Christians regard marriage as a commitment that is made to just one person for the whole of life. The husband and wife promise to care for each other, and to be loyal to each other, all through life. They also promise to share the responsibility for raising any children that they have.

In a Christian wedding, the couple make promises to each other and ask God to give them the strength to be able to keep them.

DEATH

Everyone has to die. It is sad when a friend or relative dies, and Christians feel this just as much as other people.

But they also think of death as passing from one form of existence (in this world) to another (with God). At a Christian funeral, relatives and friends will give thanks to God for the life of the person who has died. They will gather round to comfort those who are sorrowing. And they will also remind themselves of the fact that Jesus not only rose from the dead himself, but also promised his followers that they would be with him for ever.

Here is a passage from the New Testament that is often read at funerals.

Jesus said, 'I am the resurrection and the life. Those who believe in me, even though they die, will live, and everyone who lives and believes in me will never die.'

John 11:25–26

Young people mourn the death of one of their friends at the hands of death squads in Brazil. At such unhappy times, Jesus' promise that his followers will be with him forever brings comfort.

A Christian wedding is a happy event, and Is often followed by a great party.

CRISIS!

No one goes through life without having to face some problems. Sometimes these problems are very big—serious illness, abuse, divorce, or the break-up of a family—or any one of a huge range of troubles or disappointments that make people feel that the future is bleak.

There are no easy answers to these problems. But Jesus gives Christians an example to follow in helping people in such pain. He met many who were in despair and with few friends. He always cared for them, and helped them, and reminded them of God's love that never fails.

When someone does something special, it's natural to want to celebrate!

Christians see God doing special things in all the events of life, and they celebrate that all the year round.

However, the most important festivals focus on the significance of the story of Jesus and his teaching.

In some churches, these times call for a big celebration. Others make less of them. But all Christians remember the events in some way when they read the stories told about them in the Bible.

Some churches make Advent wreaths with four candles on, one more lit each Sunday of Advent. The fifth candle in the middle stands for Jesus. It is lit on Christmas Day.

ADVENT

Advent begins four Sundays before Christmas and ends on Christmas Day. 'Advent' means 'coming', and at this time Christians get ready to remember Jesus coming to this world as a baby—and their belief that he will one day return in power to bring justice at last, and to set everything right.

German carol singers, dressed as characters from the stories of the birth of Jesus, collect donations of money to help the needy. They carry a star to recall the one that led the wise men to Bethlehem.

CHRISTMAS

All Christians have special services at Christmas, many at midnight on Christmas Eve. Joyful services and special Christmas carols celebrate Jesus' birth.

For most, Christmas Day is 25 December. But some Orthodox churches use a different calendar, and celebrate Christmas on 7 January.

No one really knows when Jesus was born: the December date was chosen in the time of Constantine. There was a traditional Roman sun festival then, when people celebrated the fact that the darkest time of winter was over and the days would begin getting longer. As Christians thought of Jesus as bringing light into a dark world, it seemed a good match.

EPIPHANY

Epiphany comes twelve days after Christmas and celebrates the time when wise men from the East came to visit the infant Jesus.

The word 'Epiphany' means 'showing': Epiphany remembers the time when Jesus was shown to the wise men, who were not Jews and came from other countries far away. It reminds Christians that from the beginning Jesus was special to all peoples.

PENTECOST

Pentecost is the name of a Jewish festival that comes fifty days after Passover. At the first Pentecost after Jesus' ascension, Jesus' disciples felt the remarkable power of God's Spirit surging through them, transforming their lives forever. This power is available to all Christians all the time, to help them follow God's laws, and to care for others in the way that Jesus did.

On the first Christian Pentecost, God's spirit enabled Peter to tell a great crowd of people about Jesus, and many of those who heard decided to become followers of Jesus too. This makes the festival the church's 'birthday', and some churches have traditional birthday celebrations, such as a cake with candles on.

ASCENSION

Forty days after rising from the dead, the Gospels tell us, Jesus returned to God—and Ascension Day, always on a Thursday, celebrates that. Many churches have a special service.

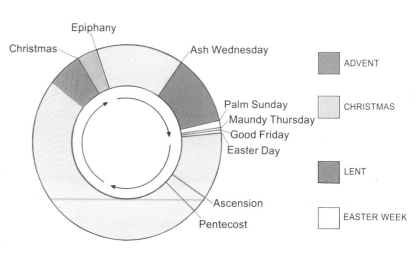

ADVENT

CHRISTMAS

LENT

EASTER WEEK

The major Christian festivals in the church year

LENT

Before Jesus began his work as a teacher, he spent forty days in the desert. It was a time of testing, when he thought about the work that lay ahead and prayed to God. Christians set aside a period of forty days each year to spend extra time praying and reading the Bible. They often make some other sacrifice, such as giving money to help people in need rather than spending it on treats for themselves, and may also decide on some positive action for good, such as spending time with someone who needs a friend. This period of forty days is called Lent.

Its first day is Ash Wednesday. In the past, people would confess the wrong they had done and put ash on their clothes as a way of expressing sorrow for their wrong-doing. Today, in some churches, the church leader makes the sign of a cross in ash on people's foreheads.

The forty days of Lent lead up to Easter.

A priest makes the sign of the cross in ash on a young Christian's forehead at an Ash Wednesday service.

EASTER

The last week leading up to Easter, Holy Week, is a great time for parades and processions, as Christians re-enact various parts of the story of Jesus' last week on earth:

Palm Sunday When Jesus came to Jerusalem for the last time to celebrate the Passover festival, he rode into Jerusalem on a donkey. Crowds waved palms to welcome him. Today, Christians may have a parade to celebrate this event, or they may hand out crosses made of palm leaves.

Maundy Thursday Jesus shared a special Passover meal with his disciples on the night before he was put to death. He told his disciples that the bread and wine were symbols of the sacrifice he was about to make for them: the broken bread like his broken body, the poured wine like his blood that would be shed. Christians celebrate this meal regularly in church, but on Maundy Thursday they think especially about that first night.

Good Friday On this day Christians remember the day Jesus died. There will sometimes be a special service from 12 noon to 3 p.m., the time when Jesus was on the cross. This service is usually very quiet, allowing people to spend time praying.

Easter Day This Sunday celebrates Jesus' rising from death. There are services with joyful singing. Some churches hold a vigil late on Saturday night, as believers gather to await the dawn of the day of Christ's resurrection. Others light a new fire early on Easter morning.

Orthodox Christians meet in complete darkness, and at midnight, the priest carries a light from the altar, from which everyone lights their own candle till the whole place is blazing with light.

Around the world, Christians meet on hillsides, beaches, and in street marches to wait for sunrise. As the day dawns, they celebrate the fact that Christ is truly alive—and that the dark power of evil has been broken for ever.

Light floods an Orthodox church on Easter Day, a symbol of Christ's victory over the dark power of evil.

A Palm Sunday procession in Jerusalem

BEING A CHRISTIAN

It's easy to see some of the things that Christians do that makes them a bit different: going to church meetings, for example, and celebrating special festivals. But there's a lot more to being a Christian than that.

Christianity is centred on God: the God who loves all people and values every one. Having God as a personal friend is what Christianity is about.

This friendship is quite different from the 'secret friend' that some small children have—just someone they make up, like a sort of invisible teddy bear! Christians will tell you that God really is there, listening to their prayers, showing them the way forward in life and helping them to do what they know is right.

That friendship gives them a courage to face life that no problems can destroy.

HOW TO BE GOD'S FRIEND

Christians say that people can be God's friends—join God's family—because of what Jesus has done. By dying on the cross he paid the price for all the wrongdoing that makes people unhappy and that cuts them off from God. He has opened up the way to God.

People who want to follow Jesus must love others in the way that God loves them. In fact, Jesus said that his disciples should be merciful—'just as your Father in heaven is merciful' (Luke 6:36).

Jesus himself set an example of great goodness, loving people whom other people had rejected and forgiving even those who put him to death.

Although Christians have made mistakes, and still do, they try their best to model themselves on Jesus, and they ask God to help them.

WHAT IS GOD LIKE?

Christians believe that they now know God. But what is God like? Here are some glimpses:

Jesus told a story about a good shepherd who looked after 100 sheep. Although 99 were safe, the shepherd could not rest and be happy until he had found the one that was lost, and brought it to safety. God is like that (Luke 15:1–7).

The Psalms in the Old Testament several times speak of God taking care of people just as a bird protects its young under its wings (Psalm 91:4).

Jesus told another story about a loving father who welcomed back his runaway son, and said that this is how God welcomes those who turn to him from their old self-centred lives (Luke 15:11–31).

In all these pictures people begin to see God as the ideal parent who cares for the little ones and always wants the best for them. Christians are members of the family of God: they are God's children, however young or old they are.

A DAY IN THE LIFE

Does it make any difference to be a Christian when it's not Sunday? Here is what one young Christian's day might be like.

Deepest night. The alarm clock rings. I put the light on. Oh, it really is morning. So I sit up.

I always try to read my Bible for a bit each day, and morning is a good time. Today I read a story Jesus told . . . about a man who got beaten up by robbers. Two religious people hurry past the scene of the crime. One, a Samaritan who the first two would have looked down on, helps out. He's clearly the one that did the right thing. So am I meant to be the one who helps others out too?

Am praying to God, thinking about this, when sister (5) pops in and asks me to read her a Bible story from her picture book. She's trying to copy me. But I do it anyway. And end up being late for breakfast, and leaving for school in tearing hurry, mess everywhere etc.

Later . . . at school, have maths class. I like maths, I'm good at it. So I help the person next to me understand the kind of stuff we're doing. We both get everything right.

Next . . . write history project book. Same person next to me has brought in loads of stuff from home to use in his. Does he let me have a look? No. Talk about unfair. Will I help him with maths next time? I guess it would still be the decent thing to do.

Lunch. I have good time with my friend. We go to the same church, and we get on, and he's pretty fair, unlike my work partner this morning. We're talking about the outing we're due to go on next weekend with the youth group . . . when there's uproar in the corner. A bunch of meanies are

terrorizing younger kids and taking their lunch. 'Come on,' says my friend. 'I'm fed up with the way those people spoil our school.'

'Help,' I mutter towards God, and we wander over. 'Now look, you lot,' says my friend, 'you are being unfair and we want you to give back what you've taken.' There are sneers and jeers from the bullies, and a look of silent fear on the face of the victims. 'Who says?' asks Bully number 1. 'We do,' I croak. It's a tense moment. They keep the food – but they do march off. 'It's not right,' says my friend. 'We've got to do something else.' And we begin to write a letter for other people to sign to tell the teachers that we want help to beat bullying.

Great afternoon. Our whole class has decided to make a wildlife area in the school grounds, so we're planting a few native trees and scattering wildflower seeds. Imagine what we've done to the world to need to scatter wildflower seeds. Yet we couldn't re-create them if we lost any species.

I went home with my friend. His mum runs a church stall selling food and other stuff bought at decent prices from developing countries so that people there get a fair wage. It makes me think how well-off we are by comparison. Unpacked loads of boxes for her into his garage – great.

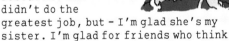

Then, home for my meal. I expected big trouble about state I left my room in this morning – but lo! Kid sister had tidied it up to rescue me. She didn't do the greatest job, but – I'm glad she's my sister. I'm glad for friends who think

the way I do. And for all that I have. So, thanks God.

God's Love

People asked Jesus what was the most important thing to do in order to live as God wants. This is his reply:

'Love the Lord your God with all your heart, with all your soul, and with all your mind.' This is the greatest and the most important commandment. The second most important commandment is like it: 'Love your neighbour as you love yourself.'

Matthew 22:34–36

You only have to look back on your life so far to realize just how much you learn as you grow up. Things that once seemed hard you can now do without a second thought.

Christians grow up in their faith too, as they learn more about God, and about how they can trust God. They discover more about what it means in practice to live as God wants.

LEARNING TOGETHER

Christians never stop learning about God. One of the most important ways is by reading the Bible.

The Bible is not particularly long, and over a lifetime people may read the same stories many times. Yet each time, new things strike them as interesting or important.

They can learn more, too, by sharing their discoveries with other Christians. That is one of the reasons Christians like to meet in small groups.

There, they will also talk about their day-to-day experiences, getting help and encouragement from one another.

And they will also have some time praying to God, because they know that God is present and cares about the whole of life.

LEARNING BY EXAMPLE

If you really want to learn how to do something, find an expert to teach you—be it a sports star or a musician.

In the same way, Christians learn from other Christians whose lives provide real inspiration—people living today, and others long ago.

Some of these people are called saints: they are remembered especially for the example they set.

Mother Teresa of Calcutta is a saintly figure from the twentieth century. She is well known for her work among the poorest of the poor in Calcutta, India. She entered a convent when she was a young woman, but when she was nearly forty she felt God was telling her to do

something else. So, with permission, she went out on her own, finding people who were dying in horrible conditions among the rubbish in the streets.

She tells of how God has provided her with what she needs to help others: buildings, food, furniture, clothing . . . and many people to help do the work, to give money to help pay for it, and to join in praying to

God. Many of those whom she has helped say that they can understand more of what God's love is like, because they have seen a glimpse of it in the love Mother Teresa has shown them.

Mother Teresa's concern is to show practical love and concern for the poorest of the poor, as if each one of them were Jesus himself.

Young Christians learning together about what the Bible teaches

TRAVELLING COMPANIONS

People often describe life as a journey, with different things to do and learn along the way. Christians—like people of other faiths—sometimes make special journeys to learn more about their faith. These journeys are called pilgrimages.

Some go to the lands where Bible events took place, and where Jesus lived. Seeing the sights and thinking about what happened there helps them to understand better, to make their faith more real, and they find this an encouragement.

Others go to places where miraculous healings are known to take place. Lourdes in France is a major pilgrimage centre because so many people have been healed when they have visited.

Being with other Christians at these times makes it possible for them to talk about their faith with a whole range of different people, and they can help encourage each other.

In some places of pilgrimage people can light candles where they are praying. The lit candle symbolizes their prayer, which God still knows about when the person stops praying.

TIME OUT

If you face difficult challenges, it's often helpful to take a break to work out how to handle them. If it's tough at school, the weekend can give you a chance to plan some survival strategies.

Christians sometimes take a break from their daily routine to have a special time of peace and quiet, where they are free to think and read more about God, and to pray.

They may go off to a quiet place on their own. It might be as simple as spending a few hours in a spare room in a friend's home! Or they might go to a place that offers this kind of special holiday: some Christian communities, such as monasteries, may have guest rooms where people can stay in peaceful surroundings and not have to talk to anyone unless they want to. Often, there will be someone in the community available for them to talk to about particular problems, who can offer support and advice.

This type of break is called a retreat.

Sometimes it helps a problem to stand back and look at it together with your friends.

Jesus showed God's love in practical ways: helping, healing, teaching and welcoming.

Christians too want to show this kind of love. There are many examples of Christians putting their love into action all over the world.

It might be a simple act of kindness, such as babysitting for someone who is feeling poorly. Or it might involve running a huge organization that brings practical help to people in needy areas anywhere in the world.

Through the centuries, Christians have often led the way in medical work, in helping the very poor and in setting up schools to train people in the skills they need to earn a better living.

The Christian faith is expressed in action. Being ready to talk about their faith is also a natural part of whatever Christians do.

Whenever you're concentrating on working hard, there isn't much time for chat. Nevertheless, Christians are always happy to talk about their relationship with God, which motivates them in everything they do. Sharing their faith often goes hand in hand with other types of work.

A good supply of clean water is essential to people everywhere. This standpipe in an African village will make life easier—and healthier—for everyone who lives there.

School can be hard work, but the education it provides gives young people a great start in life.

A Prayer About Action

This prayer, written in the sixteenth century, expresses the Christian's attitude to life and work.

> Lord Jesus,
> I give you my hands to do your work.
> I give you my feet to go your way.
> I give you my eyes to see as you do.
> I give you my tongue to speak your words.
> I give you my mind
> that you may think in me.
> Above all, I give you my heart
> that you may love, in me,
> your Father and all humankind.
> I give you my whole self,
> that you may grow in me.
> so that it is you, Lord Jesus,
> who live and work and pray in me.
>
> Lancelot Andrewes

These volunteers are giving up their summer holidays to paint and decorate a run-down children's home.

War has forced these children to flee their homes. Relief workers provide food and shelter for them at a refugee camp.

This Bangladeshi boy is learning how to run a small farm, so he will be able to earn money for his family.

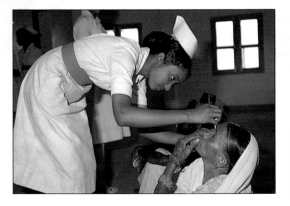

Many hospitals in the world today were originally set up by Christians.

HOPE FOR THE FUTURE

People always hope that things will turn out right ... that weather will be good on holiday, that exams will go well, that life will be interesting and rewarding.

The trouble is, things don't always go right. People suffer in all kinds of ways. Disasters may strike for no reason— earthquakes and floods may kill thousands, and leave many more with their lives in ruins. Young people as well as older ones die from illness or from silly accidents. Nations fight and kill. Harvests fail. The great, wild areas where amazing plants and animals flourished are wrecked by people who want to use the land differently, and species are wiped out for ever.

There are no easy answers. But Christians claim that their faith in Christ gives them hope, and the courage to face up to the problems.

LOOKING AFTER PEOPLE

People are very special to God, who cares for them all—rich and poor, old and young, women and men. Jesus said that people who want to follow him must show the same love: they are to love God, and to love their fellow human beings.

Christians try to show practical love and respect for every other person and to meet their needs. Many of them work particularly to help those who are poor and exploited, the lonely and those who are in despair. That kind of love makes a difference even in the most tragic situations.

LOOKING AFTER THE WORLD

Christians believe that this is the world God made, and that God wants people to look after it. It is people's selfish desire to have more and more things that has led to plundering the natural resources of the earth.

Christians—like many other people— are concerned to work to put right the damage that has been done, and to find simpler lifestyles that will mean they do not use so much of the world's resources.

The world simply isn't fair! Whilst some people have comfortable homes and lots to eat, others are forced to make their home on a rubbish tip, as at Smokey Mountain in the Philippines.

Children in Tanzania learn how to raise plants. All over the world, people need to select crops that provide good food and preserve the balance of the environment.